The Fox
the Crow

Retold by Clare Bristow

Illustrated by Paul Nicholls

Fox had been hunting all night.

There's not a bone to be seen.

I need something cold to eat.

He started to go back to his den, when ...

... he spotted Crow sitting alone in a tree.

3

Fox spied a tomato in Crow's beak.

But Fox was too far below Crow.

Fox hoped Crow might drop the tomato.

But Crow kept his beak shut.

I need him to open his beak!

Fox tried speaking to Crow.

Hello, good fellow.

But Crow did not trust Fox.

I'm not letting go of my tomato!

Crow is too smart to let go.

So, Fox tried to fool Crow.

Can you show me how you sing, Crow?

For a moment, Crow was tempted.

Crow kept his beak closed.

Next, Fox began telling Crow lies.

Fox tried one last trick.

Will you come lower so I can see those splendid black wings?

Crow stayed in the tree.

But he was tempted.

Fox is right, my wings ARE splendid.

I will show him how they glow in the sun!

So Crow swooped down low to show his wings to Fox ...

Wow! Those wings are glowing!

Thank you!

The tomato fell out of Crow's beak.

He was too slow to get it back.

Fox took hold of the big, red tomato …

… and ate the whole thing up!

Talk about the story

Answer the questions:

1 Who had been hunting all night?

2 What did Crow have in his mouth?

3 What did Fox want Crow to do?

4 How did Fox trick Crow?

5 What does it mean to trust someone?

6 Do you know any similar animal stories?

Can you retell the story in your own words?